It's My
STATE!

RHODE ISLAND

The Ocean State

Cassandra Schumacher, Rick Petreycik,
Lisa M. Herrington, and Hex Kleinmartin

Cavendish
Square

New York

Published in 2020 by Cavendish Square Publishing, LLC
243 5th Avenue, Suite 136, New York, NY 10016

Library of Congress Cataloging-in-Publication Data

Names: Schumacher, Cassandra, author.
Title: Rhode Island / Cassandra Schumacher, Rick Petreycik, Lisa M. Herrington, and Hex Kleinmartin.
Description: Fourth edition. | New York : Cavendish Square, [2020] |
Includes bibliographical references and index.
Identifiers: LCCN 2018050568 (print) | LCCN 2018050638 (ebook) | ISBN 9781502642455 (ebook) |
ISBN 9781502642448 (library bound) | ISBN 9781502644541 (pbk.)
Subjects: LCSH: Rhode Island--Juvenile literature.
Classification: LCC F79.3 (ebook) | LCC F79.3 .P48 2019 (print) | DDC 974.5--dc23
LC record available at https://lccn.loc.gov/2018050568

Editorial Director: David McNamara
Editor: Caitlyn Miller
Copy Editor: Nathan Heidelberger
Associate Art Director: Alan Sliwinski
Designer: Jessica Nevins
Production Coordinator: Karol Szymczuk
Photo Research: J8 Media

Table of Contents

SNAPSHOT
RHODE ISLAND

The Ocean State

Statehood

May 29, 1790

Population

1,059,639
(2017 census estimate)

Capital

Providence

State Seal

Rhode Island's state seal features a gold anchor on a navy background. Anchors have been a symbol of the Ocean State since the early days of the Providence Plantations. Above the anchor is the word "Hope" in all capital letters. The words around the rim of the seal say, "Seal of the State of Rhode Island and Providence Plantations 1636."

State Flag

Like the state seal, Rhode Island's flag has a gold anchor in the center. The anchor is on a bright white background and is ringed by a circle of stars. Just below the anchor is a blue ribbon with the word "Hope." The current state flag was adopted in 1897.

HISTORICAL EVENTS TIMELINE

1524

Explorer Giovanni da Verrazzano, sailing under the French flag, arrives in Rhode Island.

1635

William Blackstone becomes the first **settler** in Rhode Island.

1636

Roger Williams founds Providence as a settlement for those seeking religious freedom.

State Song

Since 1996, the state song has been "Rhode Island's It for Me." The lyrics were written by Charlie Hall, the music by Maria Day, and the arrangement is by Kathryn Chester. The song shows the state's love for its **coastline**. The chorus of the song says, "Rhode Island, oh, Rhode Island / surrounded by the sea. / Some people roam the earth for home; / Rhode Island's it for me."

State Flower

The violet was chosen as the state flower by students in 1897 and officially adopted in 1968. Violets have a pretty purple color (sometimes even blue) and sit low to the ground. Sweet-smelling common blue violets can be found across Rhode Island.

State Tree

The red maple has been the state tree since 1964 and is known for its beautiful fall colors. In autumn, the leaves of the red maple change to a variety of beautiful golds, reds, and even some deep red-purples.

1663

Rhode Island is granted a royal charter under Charles II.

1776

Rhode Island becomes the first state to declare independence from Britain.

1842

Dorr's Rebellion breaks out in Rhode Island. The rebellion lasts only a few weeks but leads to a new state constitution that gives more rights to Rhode Islanders who don't own land.

State Mineral

Bowenite

State Bird

Rhode Island Red

1994

The first WaterFire lighting takes place in Providence. WaterFire is a sculpture that consists of bonfires lit on three rivers in the city.

2011

Hurricane Irene causes power outages across the state.

2014

Gina Raimondo becomes the first woman to be elected governor of Rhode Island.

State Shell
Quahog

State Drink
Coffee Milk

CURRENT EVENTS TIMELINE

2015
The Episcopal Diocese of Rhode Island announces plans to open a slavery museum in the Cathedral of Saint John called the Center for Reconciliation.

2016
Block Island Wind Farm opens, becoming the first offshore wind farm in the nation.

2018
The nation's only rehearsal for the 2020 census is held in Providence.

Brenton Point is in Newport and offers stunning views.

1 Geography

Rhode Island may be the smallest of the fifty states, but it has a lot to offer. Rhode Islanders are proud of their state's natural beauty and its bustling cities and towns. Yet if you asked a Rhode Islander to describe their state, they'd most likely talk about the water.

No matter where you are in Rhode Island, you are never far from the ocean. It is easy to see why Rhode Island has been nicknamed the Ocean State. Sounds, bays, inlets, and the Atlantic Ocean border Rhode Island. The jagged shores along Narragansett Bay and the state's thirty-plus islands form a coastline of more than 400 miles (640 kilometers). Rhode Island also features beautiful rivers, ponds, and lakes. The landscape includes forest and hills, though Rhode Island is mainly flat.

Rhode Island's land area spans 1,034 square miles (2,678 square kilometers). About 550 Rhode Islands could fit inside the largest US state, Alaska. Because of its small size, the state is also called "Little Rhody." It's possible to drive across the entire state of Rhode Island in less than an hour. It is only 48 miles (77 km) from north to south and 37 miles (60 km) from east to west. Size is not what defines Rhode Island,

FAST FACT

Rhode Island is a small state with a big name. Its official name is the "State of Rhode Island and Providence Plantations," even after a 2010 vote to shorten the name to just "Rhode Island."

Rhode Island borders
Massachusetts
and Connecticut.

however. Its amazing people, rich history, and impressive geography are some of what makes the Ocean State a great place to call home.

How Rhode Island Was Formed

Most of Rhode Island's natural features are a result of the movement of **glaciers**, which are rivers of ice. Thousands of years ago, huge glaciers slowly expanded their reach south from Canada and covered much of the northeastern United States. As they moved, the glaciers cut into the solid rock that lay beneath loose surface material. They also helped shape hills, carrying sand, clay, and rocks.

Barden Reservoir
is located west of
Providence and provides
drinking water.

As the glaciers began to melt and retreat back toward the north, the melting ice formed rivers that washed gravel, sand, and other material onto the surrounding plains. They pushed up rocky cliffs and carved out lakes and ponds. The rushing water also created channels leading to the ocean. Natural changes to the land are responsible for many of Rhode Island's inland bodies of water. However, some of the state's water bodies are human-made lakes, or reservoirs. Altogether, there are more than three hundred reservoirs, ponds, and natural freshwater lakes in Rhode Island. The movement of glaciers formed Rhode Island's two land regions. They are the Coastal Lowlands and the Eastern New England Upland.

The Coastal Lowlands

Most of the state's major cities and tourist attractions are located in the flat Coastal Lowlands. The lowlands include the eastern section of the state and all of its islands. The Coastal Lowlands region is made up mostly of sandy beaches, saltwater ponds, marshes, and lagoons. The state's lowest point is at sea level in the lowlands.

Narragansett Bay is a stretch of water that extends north from the Atlantic Ocean and practically cuts the state in two. Narragansett Bay is connected to other smaller bays, such as Greenwich Bay and Mount Hope Bay, and many rivers, including the Providence River. East of the bay, the hills are rounded and wooded. To the west of the bay, the area has denser forests. Farther west, the ground gradually increases in elevation.

Providence is Rhode Island's capital, and it is located on the mainland near the Providence River. Other towns and cities on the mainland in the Coastal Lowlands include Warwick, Cranston, Woonsocket, Charlestown, and Westerly.

In and around Narragansett Bay are several islands. Some of these islands are home to towns and cities. Aquidneck Island, the largest island, includes Newport, Portsmouth, and Middletown. Newport is one of Rhode Island's most famous

FAST FACT

Rhode Island has more than twenty lighthouses on its shores. Lighthouses are used to help captains guide their ships back to shore and keep them from crashing or running aground. Even out-of-service lighthouses have a use. They make great tourist attractions!

Marsh Meadows Wildlife Preserve In Jamestown is a beautiful stretch of the Coastal Lowlands.

Jerimoth Hill is Rhode Island's highest point.

cities. A popular tourist destination, Newport has played a big role in the state's history.

All of the state's islands are located in, or border, Narragansett Bay except for Block Island. This popular vacation spot is the state's southernmost point. It is located in the Atlantic Ocean, about 10 miles (16 km) from the Rhode Island coast, and is only 6 miles (9.6 km) long and 3.5 miles (5.6 km) wide. It is not connected to the mainland by any bridges or tunnels. The only way to get there is by plane or boat. Ferries carry visitors to Block Island. Nature trails, historic buildings, lighthouses, and other tourist attractions are found on the island. It is also home to about eight hundred year-round residents who have their own town government, school system, and other public services.

The Eastern New England Upland

The Eastern New England Upland, which extends from Connecticut to Maine, stretches through the northern and western regions of Rhode Island. It covers about two-thirds of the state's total area. Rolling hills, narrow valleys, wooded areas, ponds, lakes, and reservoirs mark this scenic region, which is also called the Western Rocky Upland. The area has higher elevations than the Coastal Lowlands. At 812 feet (247 meters) above sea level, Jerimoth Hill is the highest point in Rhode Island.

The western portion of the state is dotted with small towns and cities, rivers, reservoirs, and lakes. Much of the land is ideal for growing hay, corn, and potatoes. The wooded areas in the region are filled with a variety of trees, including oak, maple, hickory, birch, pine, spruce, cedar, and hemlock. Parts of

Roger Williams and the Foundation of Rhode Island

Roger Williams founded Rhode Island with a strong set of beliefs. Those beliefs would later influence the Founding Fathers of America. That means Williams's ideas shaped the whole nation.

Williams believed that the Native people of Rhode Island were the rightful owners of the land. He had a great deal of respect for the Native people and treated them fairly. Williams bought the land for his settlement from the **Native Americans** who already lived there.

Williams also believed in freedom of religion and the separation of church and state. These were the founding ideas behind the Providence Plantations of Rhode Island. Williams wrote, "The civil state [must] proclaim free and impartial liberty to all the people." In other words, governments should not put one religion ahead of any other. Governments should treat people of all faiths equally. Williams believed that religious ideas should be separate from the work of running a state or country. At the time, this was a radical idea. Later, the separation of church and state became a key part of the United States Constitution. Today, it remains one of the most important American beliefs about government.

Even though Williams's ideas have stood the test of time, the borders of Rhode Island changed a lot over the years. Williams's colony was not recognized by the Dutch, who tried to claim Rhode Island. Connecticut and Massachusetts also wanted pieces of Rhode Island. Arguments with Massachusetts over Rhode Island's boundary lasted a very long time. In 1861, the US Supreme Court had to weigh in. The arguments with Connecticut lasted even longer. Because of a flawed map, confusion over the Connecticut–Rhode Island border lasted through the 2000s!

Roger Williams lived from 1603 to 1683. He founded Rhode Island in 1636.

Rhode Island's upland are perfect for those who enjoy outdoor activities such as hiking, canoeing, fishing, and horseback riding.

Climate

Rhode Island's **climate** tends to be milder than that of its New England neighbors. This means that Rhode Island usually has warmer winter temperatures. The higher temperatures are a result of the winds blowing in from the Atlantic Ocean and Narragansett Bay. The northern and northwestern sections of Rhode Island tend to have cooler year-round temperatures than southern and coastal Rhode Island. In the summer, the coast and the southern portions of the state are slightly warmer than the northern sections.

Rhode Island sometimes experiences extreme weather. In 2012, Superstorm Sandy damaged Rhode Island homes and businesses.

In general, the coldest months in the state are January and February. During January, Rhode Islanders can expect an average temperature of about 29 degrees Fahrenheit (–2 degrees Celsius). The lowest temperature in the state occurred on January 11, 1942, when the village of Wood River Junction recorded a frigid –28°F (–33°C).

The warmest months in Rhode Island are July and August. The average July temperature is 73°F (23°C). The heat became pretty intense for residents of Providence on August 2, 1975, when the temperature climbed to a record-breaking 104°F (40°C).

Precipitation is the amount of water that falls as rain, snow, or other moisture. Rhode Island's average precipitation is about 47 inches (119 centimeters) per year, though the southwestern part tends to be wetter than the rest of the state. Annual snowfall in the state amounts to about 31 inches (79 cm).

Visiting the Breakers

Rhode Island's Gilded Age homes bring visitors from all over. The Gilded Age was an era of extreme wealth during the **Industrial Revolution** of the 1800s, and some of the richest families in the United States built vacation homes in Rhode Island at that time. Together, these vacation properties are known as the Newport **Mansions**.

Perhaps the most famous of the Newport Mansions is the Breakers. Built by Cornelius Vanderbilt II in 1893, the home has seventy rooms! The Breakers became a National Historic Landmark in 1994. The Preservation Society of Newport oversees nine mansions in total, all of which are open to tourists.

Visitors can feel like royalty as they stroll through the homes. Audio tours guide tourists through the mansions and try to create a picture of what daily life would have been like for the rich and powerful people who vacationed there. Visiting is an opportunity to take a step back in time.

The Breakers was built in 1893. Today, it is a popular tourist attraction.

Hurricanes and floods have been the fiercest weather events that Rhode Islanders living in coastal areas have had to deal with over the years. Hurricanes usually strike in late summer and early fall. Strong hurricane winds can damage or destroy homes and other buildings. The heavy rains and strong, tall waves from hurricanes often cause flooding and structural damage to buildings. Throughout Rhode Island's history, hurricanes have caused millions of dollars of damage.

Wildlife

Rhode Island hosts a wide variety of plants and animals. More than 60 percent of the state is forested. Around sixty different species, or types, of trees thrive in Rhode Island. They include ashes, hickories, elms, maples, poplars, beeches, willows, birches, and Atlantic white cedars. In the warm-weather months, inland fields are often dotted with colorful wildflowers, such as goldenrod, asters, violets, and lilies. Flowering plants also populate the state's wooded areas. Among these are mountain laurels, wild roses, dogwoods, azaleas, blue gentians, orchids, irises, and rhododendrons.

Rhode Island has more than eight hundred species of animals, including beavers.

Many wild mammals roam Rhode Island's wooded areas as well. They include white-tailed deer, skunks, rabbits, raccoons, squirrels, moles, foxes, and woodchucks. Beavers, muskrats, otters, and mink can be spotted swimming in the state's ponds, rivers, and lakes. Other inhabitants of these freshwater areas include fish such as bass, perch, pike, trout, and pickerel.

The salty coastal waters are home to swordfish, striped bass, flounder, sharks, tuna, mackerel, jellyfish, bluefish, cod, and butterfish. Shellfish also thrive, particularly lobsters, soft-shell crabs, oysters, scallops, mussels, and clams.

During winter months, harbor seals can be found lounging on Block Island's rocks and beaches.

More than four hundred species of birds have been spotted in the state. Rhode Island's wooded areas are home to robins, owls, blue jays, flickers, sparrows, and catbirds. Looking for meals of fish and shellfish along the coast are seagulls, terns, osprey, and loons. Geese and ducks live near the state's waterways. Rhode Island also has some game birds, including pheasants and quails, that are hunted during specific times of the year.

The roseate tern is an endangered bird that lives along the coast.

Endangered Animals

Rhode Island has gone to great lengths to protect its wildlife. However, increasing pollution has put some types of wildlife in the state in danger of disappearing completely. When a type of animal or plant is endangered, it is at risk of dying out. A threatened species is at risk of becoming endangered. Rhode Island has several endangered species, including the roseate tern, the American burying beetle, and multiple types of sea turtles.

A Special Place

More than one million people call Rhode Island home. They enjoy the state's forests, parks, beaches, farms, and urban centers. The state has come a long way since Roger Williams established Providence. Yet Rhode Island's beauty has remained constant.

More than half of Rhode Island is forested area.

Rhode Island's Biggest Cities

(Population numbers are from the US Census Bureau's 2017 projections for incorporated cities and towns.)

Providence

Pawtucket

1. Providence: population 180,393

Founded in 1636, Providence is the state capital and one of the oldest cities in the United States. In the 1990s, the mayor spearheaded improvements such as the creation of Waterplace Park and the Providence Rink. The city is known for its art, including large public sculptures.

2. Cranston: population 81,202

In 1754, a section of Providence called Pawtuxet split away and became the town of Cranston. It became a city on March 10, 1910. Today, Cranston is home to more than 2,700 businesses and two state parks. The city is located in Providence County.

3. Warwick: population 80,871

Founded in 1642, Warwick was destroyed during King Philip's War (1675–1676). In 1772, members of the Sons of Liberty burned a British ship in Warwick during the lead-up to the American Revolution. Today, it is a place for residents to relax at freshwater or saltwater beaches.

4. Pawtucket: population 72,001

Pawtucket was founded in 1671 and is famous for producing cotton textiles during the American Revolution. Residents of Pawtucket are invested in making their city a great place to visit, live, and do business. The Pawtucket Foundation is a nonprofit committed to creating jobs in the city.

5. East Providence: population 47,600

East Providence has its origins in land purchases in 1641 and 1661 and was incorporated in 1862 as a city from "Old Seekonk." The city is actually made up of the three villages of East Providence Center, Riverside, and Rumford.

6. Woonsocket: population 41,759

Woonsocket was created by joining six villages: Bernon, Globe, Hamlet, Jenckesville, Social, and Woonsocket Falls. It was incorporated as a city in 1888. It is home to Autumnfest, an annual cultural festival held on Columbus Day weekend.

7. Coventry: population 34,933

Coventry was settled in the early eighteenth century, and there are many eighteenth- and nineteenth-century homes and farms that are still standing today. The Nathanael Greene Homestead is even open to visitors.

8. Cumberland: population 34,927

Cumberland is the northeasternmost town in Rhode Island. It was settled in 1635 and incorporated in 1746. Cumberland boasts farms, vineyards, and the Blackstone River Bikeway, Rhode Island's second-longest bike path.

Cumberland

9. North Providence: population 32,511

North Providence was founded in 1636 and incorporated as a town in 1765. At 5.6 square miles (14.5 sq km), it is the smallest town by area in the smallest state in the country. The town prides itself on being a great place to raise a family.

10. South Kingstown: population 30,788

South Kingstown dates back to 1722 and was incorporated in 1723. The town is known for its beautiful beaches. Its charming inns make visitors feel right at home.

The Plants and Animals of Rhode Island

Hickory tree

Pink lady slipper orchids

What Grows in Rhode Island?

Hickory Trees Rhode Island relied on lumber trade in colonial times, and hickory trees produce good-quality lumber. Hickory wood is still used today for making cabinets and other furniture. Hickory trees also produce nuts with very hard shells that taste similar to pecans.

Orchids Rhode Island has thirty-six orchids native to the state, but thirty-three of them are now considered rare. This means these species of orchids are at risk of dying out in the state. Ten of those rare species are already considered historic, which means they have not been seen in Rhode Island in a very long time. The only types that are not considered rare are the pink lady slipper and two kinds of rattlesnake plantain.

Red Maples The red maple is the state tree of Rhode Island and is known for its bright red and gold leaves in the fall season. Though it produces sweet sap, it is not as good for syrup making as sugar maples are. The red maple was chosen by children as the state tree in in the 1890s and became the official state tree in 1964.

Rhode Island Greening Apples Rhode Island's state fruit is the greening apple, which is one of the oldest American apples. They were often used in cooking during colonial times and likely date back to the 1650s. Greenings can be used for baking and making cider. They can last for months in cold storage, so they are enjoyed all year long.

Violets The violet was officially named the state flower in 1968. Rhode Island was the last state to choose a state flower. Violets can be eaten, but be careful because there are plants that look like violets that can be poisonous. The flower has a sweet and bright scent, and often a bright purple, nearly blue color.

What Lives in Rhode Island?

American Burying Beetle The American burying beetle was named the state bug of Rhode Island in 2015. The American burying beetle is nocturnal, which means it is awake at night and sleeps during the day. The beetle is endangered and can only be found in a few states.

American burying beetle

Harbor Seal The long Rhode Island coast is a great place to spot harbor seals. They are considered Rhode Island's state marine mammal and have been since 2016. Harbor seals weigh around 245 pounds (111 kilograms), sometimes more. Visitors to Rhode Island can spot them in Narragansett Bay when they migrate there between September and June.

Harbor seals

Rhode Island Red Chicken The Rhode Island red chicken is the state bird. This fast-growing chicken is easy to raise, hardy, and good for laying eggs. In fact, Rhode Island reds are one of the top egg producers of all the chicken breeds. They are named for their deep red feathers.

Striped Bass Striped bass can live for more than thirty years and can weigh up to 80 pounds (36 kg). Known for the silver stripes on their sides, striped bass are a prize catch for sport fishers in Rhode Island. In 2000, striped bass became the state fish of Rhode Island.

Striped bass

This illustration shows settlers on Aquidneck Island in 1641.

2 The History of Rhode Island

Modern Rhode Island has been thousands of years in the making. Long before the first Europeans reached the New World, what is today known as Rhode Island was home to people known as Paleoamericans. Their descendants are Native Americans, and Native American history is a key part of Rhode Island's story.

Early People

Many historians and scientists estimate that the first humans arrived in the region that now includes Rhode Island around 8000 BCE. These people were the Paleoamericans. They were mainly hunters and gatherers who looked for food in the area's thick forests and coastal waters. They lived in small communities, made tools out of stone, and grew crops such as corn, beans, squash, cucumbers, tobacco, and pumpkins.

In the early seventeenth century, about ten thousand Native Americans lived in the area. They belonged to four main tribes: the Nipmuc, Eastern Niantic, Wampanoag, and Narragansett. Except for occasional battles between the Narragansett (the largest and

FAST FACT

The Providence Plantations were the first European settlements in Rhode Island. This is where the second half of Rhode Island's name, State of Rhode Island and Providence Plantations, comes from.

The Native People

Tribes that lived in Rhode Island included the Narragansett (throughout the state, but mostly to the west of Narragansett Bay all the way to Connecticut), the Eastern Niantic (along the southern coast), the Nipmuc (along the northern border of the state), and the Wampanoag (along the eastern boarder of the state). All of these groups were a part of the Algonquians, a large collection of northeastern tribes that shared customs and related languages.

Native Americans were hunters and farmers by the time Europeans began to visit North America. Women harvested maize (hard corn), squash, and beans and also gathered nuts and fruit, while men did most of the hunting. They shot deer, turkeys, and small game, and went fishing, with those on the coast often fishing from dugout canoes.

Children collected other food such as berries, nuts, and herbs. In the coastal areas, people would build wigwams, or wetus, which were 8 to 10 feet (2.4 to 3 m) tall with a domed roof. These were built from a wooden pole framework and covered with birch bark and woven mats. Farther inland, people also built **longhouses**, which had straight walls and curved roofs. They could be 20 feet (6 m) wide, 20 feet (6 m) tall, and up to 200 feet (61 m) long. While the small wigwams would be comfortable for a single family for several months, the longhouses could hold many families and be permanent living spaces. Most of the Native Americans living in the region settled in villages near water, which gave them easy access to sources of food and trade. They also had a system of government in which village leaders functioned as judges and resolved legal and spiritual disputes.

The Native tribes were practically wiped out in King Philip's War. The Native Americans who remained did not have much power against the white settlers. Some moved away, while others gave up their lifestyles to fit in with the colonists. The Narragansett are the only federally recognized Native American tribe left in the state.

The Native Narragansett People

Narragansett is pronounced "nair-uh-GANN-set." It comes from the Narragansett place name Naiaganset, which means "small point of land." Currently, the Narragansett occupy the Narragansett Indian **Reservation**, 1,800 acres (728 hectares) of trust lands in Charlestown and several hundred acres in Westerly. The group has just over two thousand members, and the main community is at Charlestown. Historically, the Narragansett were known as warriors. They offered protection to the Niantic.

The Narragansett hold a powwow in Charlestown.

Homes: The Narragansett favored longhouses and wetus for their villages. Many families would live together for long periods of time.

Food: The Narragansett grew the "three sisters" of maize, squash, and beans, which were all planted together and helped each other grow. They also hunted deer, turkeys, squirrels, rabbits, and other small animals, as well as fished and gathered clams.

Clothing: Narragansett men wore breechcloths, while women wore skirts to their knees, and all wore moccasins. Shirts were not usually worn, but in colder weather people wore deerskin capes. Women usually had long hair, but men, especially warriors, might shave all but one small area of their head and keep the remaining hair long to produce a scalp lock.

Art: The Narragansett, like most coastal northeastern Native Americans, did beadwork and made wampum from shell beads that could be used for messages or as money. They also made decorative beads.

Explorer Giovanni da Verrazzano was the first European to reach Rhode Island.

most powerful group in the region) and the Wampanoag (who inhabited the far eastern parts), the tribes lived peacefully.

Europeans Arrive

The first known European to explore the area was an Italian sailing for France named Giovanni da Verrazzano, who landed near Block Island in 1524. In 1614, Dutch sea captain Adriaen Block became the next European arrival. Block Island is named after him.

In 1630, about one thousand Puritans left England to start a colony in Massachusetts. A colony is land settled and governed by another country. The Puritans had left England because they disagreed with the Church of England. They believed in firm obedience to church laws, which were strictly enforced by their colony's governor, John Winthrop.

The Wampanoag and the Narragansett helped Roger Williams after he was cast out of Massachusetts Bay Colony.

Founding Rhode Island

In 1631, Roger Williams, an English preacher, arrived in Boston. He believed in religious freedom—that individuals should be free to worship God however they desire, and that the laws of a church and of government should be separate. Williams made friends with Native Americans and respected their way of life, and he thought white settlers should treat them fairly and pay them for land taken by settlers.

Williams's beliefs conflicted with those of the Puritan leaders of the Massachusetts Bay Colony. Officials arrested him on several occasions, finally casting him out in 1635. Before Williams could be sent back to England, he fled south. In a few days, he arrived at the eastern side of Narragansett Bay, where the Wampanoag and their leader, Massasoit, welcomed him. He also met the Narragansetts.

Other white settlers seeking religious freedom soon joined Williams. In June 1636, he purchased land from Massasoit and two Narragansett leaders, Canonicus and Miantonomo. Thus, Williams created the first permanent settlement in Rhode Island. He named it Providence, as he felt that God's "watchful eye" had kept him safe and guided him on his trip from Massachusetts. Other settlements soon sprang up in the area that now includes Portsmouth, Newport, and Warwick.

In 1634, Anne Hutchinson (1591–1643) moved with her family from England to the Massachusetts Bay Colony in search of religious freedom. She challenged the religious views of Puritan leaders with her preaching. Puritan officials believed that women should not be able to preach. Like Roger Williams, Hutchinson was banned from the colony.

With the help of Williams, she and her followers founded present-day Portsmouth in Rhode Island in 1638. (Other Hutchinson followers headed south and founded Newport in 1639.) After her husband's death, Hutchinson moved to present-day New York. She was killed in 1643 during a fight with Native Americans.

Anne Hutchinson founded Portsmouth after she was banned from Massachusetts Bay Colony.

Creating a Colony

In 1644, the English Parliament granted Williams a document of rights called a charter. The charter recognized the four settlements of Providence, Portsmouth, Newport, and Warwick as the colony of Providence Plantations, which in 1647 officially united.

Representatives from each settlement met at Portsmouth. They set up a system of government that included a representative assembly and a president, who would be elected by the male residents.

By the 1650s, Roger Williams's vision of religious freedom and tolerance for all made Rhode Island a popular place for people of different faiths. In 1663, King Charles II of England granted the four settlements a new royal charter. The charter gave the colony the name Rhode Island and Providence Plantations. It provided the new colony with more self-government than any of the other colonies. The charter also allowed the colony to continue Roger Williams's "lively experiment" of freedom of religion for all.

In Providence, in 1638, Williams established the first Baptist church in what is now the United States. Another group of Christians called Quakers built a meetinghouse on Aquidneck Island in 1657. People of the Jewish faith began settling in Rhode Island in the 1650s, and in 1763, the Touro Synagogue opened in Newport. It is the oldest Jewish house of worship in the United States and is now a National Historic Site.

The Touro Synagogue is the oldest synagogue in the United States.

King Philip's War

For nearly forty years after Roger Williams founded Providence, Rhode Island's colonists had peaceful relations with the area's Native Americans. That is partly because Williams believed that, as the first inhabitants of the area, Native Americans were the rightful owners of the land and should be paid for losing it. However, settlers in other colonies started a war by taking land.

The Wampanoag leader Metacom declared war on the settlers of Rhode Island in 1675 over land rights.

In 1675, Metacom, a Wampanoag leader whom the settlers called King Philip, began attacking English settlements. He convinced other groups in the region—including members of the Nipmuc and Narragansett tribes—to join him.

At first, King Philip targeted only colonial settlements in Massachusetts Bay. That changed when militias from Connecticut and Massachusetts Bay attacked and defeated a group of warriors near a southern Rhode Island town now called Kingston. The battle became known as the Great Swamp Fight. The colonial militias did not stop there, continuing to raid and burn surrounding Native American villages. Within a few days, they had killed more than a thousand Native men, women, and children.

The first major battle of King Philip's War was the Great Swamp Fight, which took place in December 1675.

King Philip and his allies fought back, attacking settlements and setting Providence on fire. Settlers from the town and neighboring areas were forced to flee to offshore islands. In 1676, King Philip was killed in a battle near present-day Bristol, Rhode Island. The series of battles between the Native American tribes and English colonists became known as King Philip's War.

The Narragansett, Wampanoag, Nipmuc, and other tribes involved in the conflict were practically wiped out as a result of the war. Several hundred of King Philip's warriors were also captured and sold into slavery in other countries. The relationships between the Rhode Island colonists and the region's Native Americans were never the same.

Colonial Trading

The early 1700s marked the beginning of a period of great wealth for Rhode Island. The colony's **population** grew from just seven thousand people in 1710 to forty thousand in 1755. Farming and whaling were very profitable businesses. Candles and other products were made from whale oil. Through sea trading, the colony's merchants sold and traded everything from wood, salt, cider, dairy products, and molasses to

Whaling enriched colonists but was very dangerous.

horses, fish, and preserved meats. Rhode Island's coasts made it easy for ships to come in and sail out carrying a wide variety of goods. Within a short period of time, Newport and Providence emerged as bustling ports in colonial America.

Rhode Island merchants also made a lot of money from the slave trade. In fact, they controlled between 60 and 90 percent of the American trade in African slaves. Rhode Island's wealth during this period depended on its position in the Triangle Trade, a trade route whose three points were Rhode Island, Africa, and the Caribbean Islands, also known as the West Indies.

Rhode Island merchants would send rum made in Rhode Island using molasses from the West Indies to Africa. Once the rum arrived in Africa, it was exchanged for enslaved Africans. The enslaved people were shipped to the West Indies to work on the sugar plantations. They were traded for molasses produced from the sugar. The molasses was then sent to Rhode Island and turned into more rum.

Slave ships were dirty and crowded. Many enslaved people died from the horrible conditions. Some enslaved people from Africa ended up working in Rhode Island. By 1774, enslaved people made up more than 6 percent of Rhode Island's population. In 1784, Rhode Island passed a law that freed the children of enslaved people. The international slave trade, however, continued into the 1800s.

The Lead-Up to the American Revolution

In the late 1600s through the 1700s, Great Britain was involved in a series of wars with France for control over much of North America. The last of these struggles is known as the French and Indian War (1754–1763). Great Britain defeated France, gaining almost all of France's land east of the Mississippi River. Great Britain expected its colonies to provide troops, and even after the fighting was over, Britain imposed fees and taxes on the colonists to help pay for the war.

The French and Indian War lasted from 1754 to 1763.

Many colonists, however, disagreed with the new British taxes, feeling the war debt was Britain's responsibility. In 1764, the British Parliament passed the Sugar Act, requiring the colonists to pay a tax on imported goods such as molasses, sugar, and wine. The next year, the British Parliament passed the Stamp Act, which taxed all paper items—from legal documents to playing cards—in the colonies. The colonists were angered even further.

In protest and to avoid paying taxes, some merchants smuggled molasses, sugar, and other taxable goods into the colony, and the general unrest eventually led to violence. In 1769, colonists burned the British ship *Liberty* in Newport's waters, and on June 10, 1772, a group of Providence merchants lured a British customs ship (there to collect taxes) called the *Gaspee* into Narragansett Bay and set it on fire. The *Gaspee*'s commander was shot and wounded during the colonists' attack. These events in Rhode Island were some of the first acts of colonial rebellion against Great Britain.

Rhode Island's Revolutionaries

In the spring of 1775, colonists in Massachusetts fought British troops at Lexington and Concord, beginning the American Revolution. Rhode Island immediately sent troops to help its neighbor fight the British. In June, George

Washington was named the leader of the Continental Army that would bring together soldiers from all of the thirteen colonies.

Washington was named the army's leader by the Second Continental Congress, which included representatives from the thirteen colonies. Rhode Island's delegates suggested starting an American fleet, and the Continental Navy was established in October 1775. Stephen and Esek Hopkins, brothers from Rhode Island, helped create the Continental Navy. Esek Hopkins became its first commander in chief.

On May 4, 1776, Rhode Island became the first New England colony to declare independence from Great Britain. Two months later, on July 4, 1776, delegates to the Continental Congress from all thirteen colonies approved the Declaration of Independence, stating that "these United Colonies are, and of Right ought to be, Free and Independent States."

The American Revolution included many battles throughout the colonies, and Rhode Island soldiers took part in the fighting. Residents in the colony who supported independence also provided supplies, money, and food for the troops. In August 1778, one of the largest land battles of the American Revolution, known as the Battle of Rhode Island, took place near Newport. General Nathanael Greene, a Rhode Islander, led American troops during the battle.

Nathanael Greene, a Rhode Island general, led troops in the Battle of Rhode Island and the Battle at Yorktown.

Also fighting in the Battle of Rhode Island was a group of soldiers called the Black Regiment of Rhode Island. They formed the first African American army unit. The unit was made up of more than 120 black men, including about 100 enslaved Africans.

Greene played a key role in the final British defeat. Under his leadership, American troops in the South forced a British army led by General Cornwallis to retreat to Yorktown,

Virginia, in 1781. There, George Washington and his troops, supported by French forces, trapped and attacked Cornwallis's army and forced the British to surrender.

In 1783, the former thirteen colonies signed a peace agreement with Great Britain called the Treaty of Paris, in which Britain officially accepted American independence. In 1787, the Constitution of the United States of America was drafted at a convention in Philadelphia. The document outlined how the US government would operate and what powers it would have. Each state had to ratify (approve) the Constitution.

Rhode Islanders were concerned about giving up too much power to the federal government, however. They refused to ratify the Constitution until it included additional rights that would protect individual liberties and limit federal authority. Finally, the US Congress approved the first ten amendments to the Constitution, called the Bill of Rights. On May 29, 1790, Rhode Island approved the US Constitution.

At the Constitutional Convention in Philadelphia, colonial leaders wrote the Constitution.

The Industrial Revolution Begins

In the late 1700s and into the 1800s, Rhode Island's **economy** boomed due to the Industrial Revolution, when **manufacturing** became a major **industry** in the state. A Providence merchant who had been operating a mill that spun cotton in Pawtucket visited Great Britain. He witnessed how British cotton mills used water-powered machines to spin cotton into thread. These machines allowed the British mills to produce goods faster and cheaper. The merchant wished to know how to build and run such machines, but British mill owners kept it

The Providence Tool Company was one of Rhode Island's early manufacturers.

Rhode Island Independence Day

Rhode Island has many holidays in common with its fellow states, but it has one very special holiday all to itself. On May 4 every year, Rhode Islanders show their patriotism and celebrate Rhode Island Independence Day.

While all the other states declared independence from England through the Declaration of Independence on July 4, 1776, Rhode Island had already declared independence two months earlier. On May 4, 1776, Rhode Island's government passed a law declaring the colony as an independent state.

Rhode Island Independence Day is a state holiday, which means government and municipal offices close while stores and many businesses stay open. It is a day for picnics and other celebrations, and it is often used as a day to show appreciation for the military.

Rhode Island was the first state to declare independence from Britain in 1776.

a secret from people in other countries. In fact, anyone who worked in a water-powered mill in Great Britain was forbidden to leave the country.

However, one mill worker did manage to slip out without getting caught. Samuel Slater disguised himself as a farmer, boarded a ship, and ended up in Pawtucket in 1790. Slater worked with the merchant, Moses Brown, to re-create a water-powered mill similar to those in Great Britain. The rolling Blackstone River was the perfect source for a waterwheel. In 1793, Slater created the first water-powered cotton mill in the United States.

Within a few years, other mills sprang up along Rhode Island's many rivers. Textiles (cloth) became a leading industry for the state. The use of water to power mills was also applied to other industries. Pawtucket's David Wilkinson developed a water-powered mill to manufacture metal tools and equipment, shifting the economy from farming and sea trading to manufacturing.

In 1794, two brothers, Nehemiah and Seril Dodge, started making costume jewelry in Providence. They found a way to cover cheaper metals with better-looking and more expensive metals. With this innovation, Rhode Island entered the jewelry industry. By 1824, Providence had become the jewelry-making capital of North America.

In the 1830s, silversmith Jabez Gorham began manufacturing sterling silver. It is a pure silver melted with another metal, often copper, to make it stronger. At first, Gorham made spoons, thimbles, and jewelry. In time, his son, John, made the Gorham Manufacturing Company

Gorham silverware has been manufactured in Rhode Island since the 1830s.

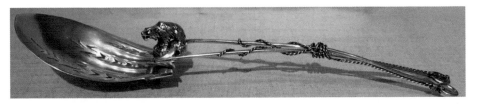

into the largest sterling silver manufacturer in the world. Many US presidents have served their guests using Gorham silverware.

From the 1840s through the 1850s, railroad lines began to cross through Rhode Island. The railroads helped connect Rhode Island to other states, making it cheaper for Rhode Island's factories to ship their products around the country, which made manufacturing more profitable.

As word of the state's wealth spread, it began to attract people from other countries seeking better opportunities. Soon, a steady stream of **immigrants** made their way into the state. Rhode Island's population skyrocketed from just under 70,000 in 1800 to almost 148,000 in 1850.

Demands for Change

In 1841, a Providence attorney named Thomas Dorr tried to change the state's outdated charter, starting a movement known as the Dorr Rebellion. Dorr and his supporters drafted a new constitution that extended voting rights to all adult males who lived within the state. His supporters held their own statewide election and elected Dorr as their governor in 1842. However, he was arrested, convicted of treason, and sentenced to life in prison. (He was released after serving only a year.) The Dorr Rebellion led to a revised state constitution in 1843. The change allowed males, including African Americans, who were born in the United States to vote without owning property if they could pay a one-dollar poll tax.

Water mills were a key part of the Industrial Revolution in Rhode Island. They were powered by waterwheels. It's easy to make your own waterwheel at home.

Make Your Own Waterwheel

Supplies

- 1 large plastic disposable cup
- 1 straw
- 1 empty plastic spool of thread
- 1 empty soda bottle
- 1 metal washer
- Duct tape
- Thread
- Scissors

Directions

1. Cut through the middle of the cup and around the outside to make a strip of plastic that is as wide as the empty spool.
2. Cut this strip of plastic into six quarter-inch strips. These are your blades.
3. Duct tape one long edge of each strip to the spool. All the curves of all the blades need to face the same direction and out from the spool like spokes on a wheel.
4. Slide the straw through the middle hole of the spool.
5. Tape the spool to the straw.
6. Tape the thread to the far side of the straw.
7. Tie your metal washer to the other end of the thread.
8. Ask an adult to cut the top off the soda bottle all the way around and make two equal notches in opposite sides of the bottle.
9. Place the straw in the notches so that the spool is in the middle. The curved blades should be facing up.
10. Place the bottle under a faucet so the water hits the "wings" of your wheel. You will not need a lot of water.
11. Watch as the energy created by the spinning wheel winds the thread and pulls up the washer!

Rhode Island's Role in the Civil War

Not long after Abraham Lincoln was elected the sixteenth US president in 1860, the Civil War (1861–1865) broke out. This conflict bitterly divided the Northern and Southern states, which disagreed on slavery and other issues. Most Northerners opposed slavery, while many Southerners believed they had the right to own slaves.

Southern states feared Lincoln's election would lead to restrictions on or even the abolition (end) of slavery. By early 1861, eleven Southern states had decided to break away from the United States and form a new government called the Confederate States of America. The other states went to war to bring the Confederate states back into the Union.

Rhode Island manufacturers had been buying a great deal of cotton from Southern states to keep their textile mills running, so they did not want to fight against the Confederacy. Eventually, though, Rhode Island contributed more than twenty-four thousand troops to the Union army. The state's factories and farms provided supplies and food for Union troops.

After years of fighting and the loss of hundreds of thousands of lives, the Confederacy surrendered in 1865. Then the Thirteenth Amendment to the US Constitution was adopted, outlawing slavery throughout the United States.

The Industrial Era

Rhode Island's economy and population continued to grow after the Civil War. The state's textile mills produced thread, yarn, cotton shirts, and other goods, which were then shipped to countries all over the world. Rhode Island's jewelry and metal products industries were also flourishing.

This economic prosperity set the stage for a period in the late 1800s known as the Gilded Age. During this time, many of the country's richest families, such as the Astor, Vanderbilt, Morgan, and Belmont families, chose to spend summers in Newport. Members of these elite families, most of them based in New York, were famous business leaders who made huge fortunes in manufacturing, transportation, and banking. They built stunning seaside mansions located on Newport's Bellevue Avenue, many of which have been designated National Historic Landmarks.

Other mansions, such as Hammersmith Farm, built in 1887, have been turned into private residences. The wedding reception of Jacqueline Bouvier and John F. Kennedy was held at Hammersmith Farm in 1953. Jacqueline spent summers as a child in the twenty-eight-room Victorian mansion. During President Kennedy's time in office, Hammersmith Farm became known as the Summer White House due to his frequent visits.

John F. Kennedy and Jacqueline Bouvier held their wedding reception at Hammersmith Farm.

Modern Times

In the 1900s, immigrants were drawn to Rhode Island's industrial success. Most of the immigrants came from Italy, Ireland, Great Britain, Portugal, Russia, Poland, and French-speaking areas of Canada. In Providence alone, the population soared from about 55,000 in 1865 to more than 175,000 in 1900. By 1925, Providence's population reached an all-time peak of 267,918.

Factory workers put in long hours in buildings that were cold during the winter and hot during the summer. Some of the machinery was dangerous, and workers

Factories, like this fish processing plant in Tiverton, brought immigrants to Rhode Island in the early twentieth century.

Important Rhode Islanders

Prudence Crandall

Prudence Crandall

Prudence Crandall was a teacher from Hopkinton, Rhode Island. Crandall advocated for the education of African American girls in Connecticut. There were many local protests against her allowing an African American girl to attend her school with white children in 1833. In response, Crandall opened a new school for young African Americans on the same grounds as her original school.

Jabez Gorham

Jabez Gorham was a silversmith from Rhode Island. Alongside Henry Webster, Gorham started the Gorham Manufacturing Company in 1831 in Providence. Gorham's company quickly became popular. Today, it is still one of the world's leading manufacturers of sterling silver flatware.

Nathanael Greene

Revolutionary War hero Nathanael Greene was born in Warwick, Rhode Island. Greene served in the Continental Army as a general during the war under George Washington. Greene became the leader of the Southern army at the end of the war.

Anne Hutchinson

Anne Hutchinson was born in Lincolnshire, England, in 1591 and later moved to the American colonies. She was a deeply religious woman. Hutchinson declared her belief that religion could be personal and required an individual relationship with God rather than one overseen by a church. Her fellow Puritans disagreed with this idea. With the support of Roger Williams, Hutchinson left Boston and founded the city of Portsmouth, Rhode Island, with her family. Hutchinson is the first woman to have founded a town in the United States of America.

H. P. Lovecraft

Howard Phillips Lovecraft (H. P. Lovecraft) was a horror and science fiction writer born in 1890 in Providence, Rhode Island. His work was often set in New England and is still read widely today.

H. P. Lovecraft

Horace Mann

Born in Massachusetts in 1796, Horace Mann went to Rhode Island at the age of twenty to attend Brown University. It was during his time there that Mann learned a great deal about politics and education. Mann went on to advocate for free public education taught by qualified teachers. Today, he is considered the father of the American public education system.

Samuel Slater

Samuel Slater was a businessman from England who memorized plans for the latest textile mills being used in England at the start of the industrial era. Slater brought the plans to Pawtucket, Rhode Island, where he started the city's first textile mill. The mill was the beginning of America's Industrial Revolution.

Horace Mann

Gilbert Stuart

Rhode Islander Gilbert Stuart was a portrait painter who painted some of the most famous Founding Fathers. John Adams, Thomas Jefferson, James Madison, and George Washington are just some of the one thousand people he painted over his lifetime. The image of George Washington on the dollar bill is based on an unfinished Gilbert Stuart painting.

Gilbert Stuart

often suffered injuries. Even children went to work in factories and mills to help their families earn money. In the early 1900s, some reforms, or changes, were made to try to protect workers from the most dangerous conditions. But the average working family still had a very difficult time making a living.

When the United States entered World War I in 1917, Rhode Island provided supplies and troops. By the time the war ended in 1918, several of Rhode Island's industries were no longer as profitable. Many of the state's textile companies had moved their mills to southern states where laborers would work for lower wages.

Things grew worse for the Ocean State during the Great Depression, which began when the stock market collapsed in 1929. Many people lost all their money. Businesses closed, and thousands of people were put out of work. Rhode Island's once-thriving textile industry had practically disappeared.

The economy began to improve during World War II. American factories reopened in 1941, manufacturing goods for the war effort. Rhode Island's factories produced ammunition, chemicals, machinery, electronics, and other war materials. US troops used metal shelters called Quonset huts (developed at the Quonset Point Naval Air Station in Rhode Island) for storage, housing, and medical centers. About ninety-two thousand Rhode Islanders served in the armed forces in World War II.

Once the war was over, Rhode Island's difficult economic times returned. Unemployment became very high. To replace the declining textile industry, efforts were made to attract other businesses. Companies specializing in electronic equipment, plastics, machinery, chemicals, health-care products, and toys began moving into the state.

In the twenty-first century, Rhode Island remains a popular vacation spot. Unfortunately, like the rest of the country, the state suffered difficult times after a severe nationwide economic recession began at the end of 2007. Many people lost their jobs. By June 2014, Rhode Island was tied with Mississippi for the highest unemployment rate (7.9 percent) of any US state.

Within the last few years, however, Rhode Island's economy has stabilized. Old factories in Providence's former jewelry district have been converted into grand buildings in the new Knowledge District. Rhode Island's focus now is on recruiting jobs in health care and other "knowledge-based" industries. Brown University opened a $45 million medical school there.

Every year, tourists flock to Rhode Island to enjoy the coast and the state's beaches.

By late 2018, the unemployment rate had dropped to around 4 percent. Both national funding and local funding were being invested into Rhode Island's economy. State government stressed the importance of job creation. Lawmakers looked for new opportunities, dedicating $135 million in state funds in 2017 to creating new jobs. Lawmakers also passed a series of tax credits to help draw in new business, including global companies, local small firms, and hotel developers.

Rhode Island continues to look to the future. One exciting project is the Block Island Wind Farm. In 2016, the wind farm opened, becoming the first offshore wind farm in the United States. Building the wind farm created many jobs, and its operation continues to employ Rhode Islanders. Rhode Island has always been a history-making state.

The Block Island Wind Farm was the first offshore wind farm in the United States.

Rhode Islanders enjoy
Newport's attractions.

3 Who Lives in Rhode Island?

Rhode Island was founded by people with big ideas. Roger Williams wanted a home where people could worship as they chose. Rhode Islanders were the first to declare independence from Great Britain. Later, the people of Rhode Island insisted on adding the Bill of Rights to the US Constitution. Rhode Islanders have a history of carving their own path.

Immigrating to Rhode Island

Before the first Europeans arrived, Native Americans inhabited the area that now includes Rhode Island. Many Europeans eventually came to the region looking for new land and religious freedom. Until the early 1800s, most of these new settlers made their living by farming, fishing, shipbuilding, and trading.

As new technologies developed, manufacturing became the center of Rhode Island's economy. Factories sprang up quickly in the state's major cities. With the increase in factories came the need for more people

FAST FACT

In 1824, female textile mill workers in Pawtucket went on strike. During a strike, people stop working to convince their employer to meet their demands. The Pawtucket work stoppage is believed to be the first strike by women workers in the United States.

Construction of Rhode Island's railroads provided jobs for immigrants.

to work in them. Rhode Island became a magnet for European and other immigrants, attracting a steady stream of people from a wide variety of backgrounds and nationalities. The Irish began immigrating to Rhode Island in the 1820s. They worked in factories and helped build the state's railroads.

During the 1860s, people from Canada as well as Germany, Sweden, Portugal, and the Cape Verde Islands off the west coast of Africa made their way to the state. Many of the Portuguese immigrants were skilled sailors. When they arrived in Newport and Providence during the 1860s, they found work on Rhode Island's whaling ships. Descendants of these workers still live in areas such as Providence's Fox Point community.

A large number of French Canadians moved to the northern city of Woonsocket during the mid-1800s. They left Quebec in Canada to work

The Rhode Island Dialect

According to the American Immigrant Council, "More than one in eight Rhode Islanders was born in another country." Even more are descended from immigrants. This fact, combined with Rhode Island's unique New England location, has created a regional **dialect** all its own.

The Rhode Island accent sounds like a mix of a Boston and Southern accent, with some Italian and Portuguese influences. It's no surprise to see the impact of Italian and Portuguese on Rhode Island. It is estimated that about 18 percent of Rhode Island's population identify as Italian American. The heaviest concentration of Italian Americans live in Johnston. The Portuguese came in the 1860s, and it's estimated that about 9 percent of Rhode Islanders identify as Portuguese American.

Atwells Avenue is Providence's "Little Italy."

According to the New England Historical Society, the Boston and Rhode Island accents are close but not the same. Bostonians stretch out the "a" in words. An example of this is the phrase "park the car." It sounds more like "pahk the cah" in Boston, while Rhode Islanders add a slight "aw" sound. With a Rhode Island accent, the phrase sounds more like "pawk the cawh."

Regional slang adds to the Rhode Island dialect. "Wicked" is used to show extra excitement or enthusiasm, like "Coffee milk is wicked good." Water fountains are known as "bubblers," and traffic circles (or roundabouts) are known as "rotaries."

Woonsocket's industrial past is celebrated at the Museum of Work and Culture.

in Woonsocket's mills and factories, producing rubber, cotton cloth, and machines. Many of their descendants are still in Woonsocket. They often speak to one another in French. French Canadians make up Woonsocket's largest ethnic group today. Woonsocket's Museum of Work and Culture tells the story of French Canadian immigrants who came to work in the city.

In the 1890s and early 1900s, immigrants arrived from Italy, Greece, Russia, Poland, Syria, Lithuania, Armenia, Lebanon, and Ukraine. In the 1970s, many Puerto Ricans, Colombians, Mexicans, Dominicans, and Guatemalans made Rhode Island their home. In addition, people from Vietnam, Cambodia, and China immigrated to Rhode Island. No matter where they are from, Rhode Islanders bring their cultures, religions, and traditions to enrich the state.

FAST FACT

Many superstars have ties to the Ocean State. Academy Award–winning actress Viola Davis was raised in Central Falls. Actress Debra Messing grew up in East Greenwich, and Taylor Swift owns a $17 million mansion in Watch Hill.

Today's Population

According to 2017 census estimates, Rhode Island has 1,059,639 residents. Among the states, Rhode Island ranks forty-third in population. Rhode Island is the second most crowded, or densely populated, state in the country, however. An average of 1,025 people live in each square mile of land (396 people per sq km).

A lack of job opportunities has affected Rhode Island's population numbers. In fact, Rhode Island is one of the slowest-growing states. Its population in 2010 had inched up by just 4,248 residents—a 0.4 percent increase—since 2000. The only state with a lower growth rate than Rhode Island from 2000 to 2010 was Michigan. Many international people continue to choose Rhode Island when relocating, so while other states' populations have

Rhode Island greening apples are the state fruit, and they taste great in desserts. Make your own apple crisp with Rhode Island greening apples if possible. If you can't get your hands on them, swap in Granny Smith apples instead.

Make Your Own Apple Crisp

Ingredients

- 4 cups of peeled and sliced apples
- ½ cup flour
- ½ cup white sugar
- 1 teaspoon cinnamon
- ½ teaspoon salt
- ½ cup slow-cooking oats
- ½ cup brown sugar
- ¼ teaspoon baking soda
- ¼ teaspoon baking powder
- ¼ cup butter (keep it in the refrigerator until you're ready to use it!)

Directions

1. Preheat your oven to 350 degrees Fahrenheit (175°C).
2. Put the apples in a large bowl. Cover the apples in 2 tablespoons flour, the white sugar, cinnamon, and salt.
3. Cover an 8×8 baking dish in tin foil. Then, place your apple mixture in the dish.
4. Mix the brown sugar, oats, baking soda, baking powder, and the remaining flour in a bowl. Use a potato masher or a fork to crumble in the butter.
5. Spread your oatmeal topping over the apple mixture in the baking dish.
6. Bake for 30 minutes or until your crisp is golden.
7. Enjoy!

decreased since 2010, Rhode Island has seen a continued, if slow, increase in population.

Most people in Rhode Island reside in urban areas. Rhode Island's five most populous cities are Providence, Cranston, Warwick, Pawtucket, and East Providence. These cities are located in the eastern section of the state. The rest of Rhode Islanders are spread out among the small, outlying rural communities.

Diversity in Rhode Island

Most Rhode Islanders trace their ancestry to Europe. Over the years, however, people with other backgrounds have settled in the state.

Hispanic Americans make up the state's largest and fastest-growing minority. In 2000, there were 90,820 Hispanic Rhode Islanders. They made up 8.7 percent of the state's population. That number rose to 130,655 in 2010, when Hispanics made up 12.4 percent of the population. That was an increase of more than 40 percent.

According to 2017 census estimates, the state has become even more diverse. Around 15 percent of the population identified as Hispanic or Latino in 2017. Many of Rhode Island's Latino residents live in communities in Providence, the state's capital and largest city. Today, African Americans comprise about 8.2 percent of the state's population. Additionally, the state's Asian population has risen to 3.7 percent.

Native People Today

Before European settlement, the region's population was Native American. Today, however, Native Americans number only about 10,000. About 2,400 belong to the Narragansett group. The tribe's headquarters

William Blackmon

Will Blackmon was born in Providence in 1984. After playing for Boston College, Blackmon was drafted into the NFL. Between 2006 and 2016, he played for the Green Bay Packers, New York Giants, Jacksonville Jaguars, and Washington Redskins. In 2018, Blackmon joined the Saskatchewan Roughriders, a Canadian Football League team.

Pauly D

Paul DelVecchio is better known as DJ Pauly D. He is a reality television star most famous for his role on MTV's *Jersey Shore* shows. In addition to his work on TV, Pauly D tours the world as a DJ. He was born in Providence in 1980.

Paul Konerko

Rhode Island native Paul "the King" Konerko is a former Chicago White Sox baseball star and World Series champion. Konerko played for the White Sox for fifteen years after being drafted by the Los Angeles Dodgers and a brief stint on the Cincinnati Reds. He retired from baseball in 2014.

Cormac McCarthy

Cormac McCarthy is the author of ten novels and has won some of the biggest prizes in literature, including the Pulitzer Prize for Fiction and the National Book Award. Several of McCarthy's books have been adapted into major films. McCarthy was born in Providence in 1933.

Meredith Vieira

Journalist and talk show host Meredith Vieira was born in Providence in 1953 and raised in East Providence. She has hosted many popular talk shows, including *The View* and the *Today* show. From 2014 to 2016, Vieira hosted *The Meredith Vieira Show*. She has won fourteen Emmy Awards.

Rhode Island's Celebrities

Will Blackmon

Pauly D

Paul Konerko

Meredith Vieira

People like Narragansett Indian tribal councilman Randy Noka are working to protect the interests of the Narragansett Tribe.

is located on a reservation in Charlestown in southern Rhode Island.

The Narragansett Indians sued the state in the 1970s to regain their lands. They were awarded about 1,800 acres (700 hectares) near Charlestown. In 1983, they gained federal recognition as the Narragansett Indian Tribe of Rhode Island.

On the reservation, the tribe keeps its heritage alive through traditional crafts, songs, storytelling, an annual powwow, and other celebrations. People can also visit the Royal Indian Burial Ground in Charlestown. It is the resting place of many Narragansett sachems (chiefs) and their families.

Rhode Island's Education System

Education is important to Rhode Islanders. The state's public education system began in the

1820s. Today, many people work for the state's school system.

Some of Rhode Island's universities are also among the state's largest employers. The main campus of the state's public university, the University of Rhode Island (URI), is located in Kingston. URI began as an agricultural school in 1888. Today, more than fifteen thousand undergraduate students are enrolled there. The school has one of the nation's leading centers for ocean research and exploration.

Rhode Island has a strong public education system and is well respected for its schools and universities.

Established in Newport in 1747, the Redwood Library and Athenaeum was the first library in Rhode Island, and it is the oldest lending library in the United States. In a lending library, members pay fees to access materials. One of Redwood's most famous librarians, Ezra Stiles (1727–1795), helped found Brown University in Providence. He later became the president of Yale University in New Haven, Connecticut.

Providence is home to several other colleges and universities. Brown graduates include actress Emma Watson, radio host Ira Glass, and business tycoon John D. Rockefeller Jr. Other schools in Providence include Providence College, Johnson and Wales University (known for its culinary arts program), and the Rhode Island School of Design (RISD). The RISD Museum contains an impressive collection of art pieces from around the world, including the work of African American landscape

This Rhode Island seascape was painted by Edward Mitchell Bannister in 1856.

artist Edward Mitchell Bannister, who painted in Rhode Island during the 1800s.

Located in Bristol is Roger Williams University. The school was named after Rhode Island's founder. Newport is home to Salve Regina University and the US Naval War College, which trains naval officers.

Proud to Call Rhode Island Home

For a small state, Rhode Island has a large population. Rhode Islanders have diverse backgrounds and experiences of living in the Ocean State. The state has great schools, a rich arts scene, and scenic coasts, but it is the people of the state who make Rhode Island what it is today. From the first residents to the Rhode Islanders of today, Rhode Island's people proudly come together to make their communities strong.

1. University of Rhode Island, Kingston

(15,092 undergraduate students)

2. Johnson & Wales University, Providence

(7,710 undergraduate students)

3. Rhode Island College, Providence

(7,080 undergraduate students)

4. Brown University, Providence

(6,988 undergraduate students)

5. Roger Williams University, Bristol

(4,703 undergraduate students)

6. Providence College

(4,306 undergraduate students)

7. Bryant University, Smithfield

(3,477 undergraduate students)

8. New England Institute of Technology, East Greenwich

(2,377 undergraduate students)

9. Salve Regina University, Newport

(2,180 undergraduate students)

10. Rhode Island School of Design, Providence

(1,976 undergraduate students)

Rhode Island's Biggest Colleges and Universities

(Enrollment numbers are from *US News and World Report* 2019 college rankings.)

University of Rhode Island

Brown University

Providence College

Bannister's Wharf in Newport is a popular tourist destination that offers quaint New England charm, art galleries, shops, and delicious dining options.

4 At Work in Rhode Island

Like many states, Rhode Island faces economic challenges. In the twenty-first century, the economy of the United States made big shifts. Manufacturing used to be the foundation of the US economy. Today, the economy centers on the service industry. Workers in the service industry help other people. They work for restaurants, retail stores, and transportation companies. Rhode Islanders are exploring new opportunities as the economy changes. Rhode Islanders are focused on bringing emerging jobs in biotechnology and other high-tech fields to the state.

Manufacturing

After Samuel Slater built his water-powered cotton mill in Pawtucket, Rhode Island quickly became a manufacturing giant. Textile mills were soon lining the state's rivers. During the entire nineteenth and early twentieth centuries, manufacturing was the most profitable industry in Rhode Island. More than half the state's workforce was employed in factories and mills. Today, however, there are fewer manufacturing jobs in the state. Although many factories have

FAST FACT
Rhode Island has a proud history of manufacturing textiles, and that tradition carries on today. In 2018, the Rhode Island Textile Innovation Network officially launched. The group is made up of government officials, textile manufacturers, and experts in the field. The network hopes to make new opportunities for Rhode Islanders.

Manufacturing plants, such as this submarine plant in North Kingston, are still an important part of the state economy.

This Townsend-Goddard table is part of the Metropolitan Museum of Art's collection.

closed or relocated, the manufacturing industry still employs about forty-one thousand people. Those workers make up about 7.3 percent of the state's labor force.

Rhode Islanders manufacture electrical supplies like light bulbs and surge protectors. They also produce computer technology like microchips and electronics. Other manufactured products include chemicals, plastics, textiles, transportation equipment, and scientific equipment—particularly medical and surgical products. Yachts, boats, and some submarine parts are also made in Rhode Island. In addition, Rhode Island is known for producing jewelry and silverware. Providence was historically home to many jewelry manufacturing companies, though their numbers have significantly declined in the twenty-first century.

In the mid-1700s, Newport was a major furniture-making center. Two of colonial America's best-known furniture makers— the Townsend and Goddard families—lived and worked in Easton's Point, a Quaker neighborhood in Newport. Many of their best-known pieces were made from mahogany wood imported from the West Indies.

Today, Newport furniture from the eighteenth century is very valuable. Many world-class museums include Townsend-Goddard pieces in their collections. In 1989, a mahogany Goddard desk and bookcase made in the 1760s sold for more than $11 million. At the time, it was the highest price ever paid for a piece of American furniture.

Mr. Potato Head, a Famous Rhode Islander

Mr. Potato Head was born in Rhode Island. The toy company Hasbro has its headquarters in Pawtucket, Rhode Island, and Mr. Potato Head is one of the most famous toys ever produced there. A member of the National Toy Hall of Fame, Mr. Potato Head was created by George Lerner and went into production in 1952.

In 1953, Mr. Potato Head's family grew. Mrs. Potato Head hit the market, along with Yam and Spud, their children. Over the years, all kinds of special Mr. Potato Head and Mrs. Potato Head toys have been sold.

Rhode Islanders love Mr. Potato Head, a claim to fame for the Ocean State. Locals can even order special license plates with images of the iconic toy stamped on them. Large statues of Mr. Potato Head dressed in different costumes can be found all over the state, including outside the Hasbro headquarters.

Mr. Potato Head is a state icon and one of Hasbro's most famous and successful toys.

This farm in Johnston grows tulips.

Agriculture

Farming, raising livestock, and fishing make up a very small part of Rhode Island's economy today. Less than 1 percent of Rhode Island's labor force works in these areas. Still, agriculture adds $100 million to the state's economy each year.

Rhode Island's top farm products are nursery and greenhouse plants. These include flowering plants, Christmas trees, grass sod, and decorative trees and shrubs. Rhode Island farm crops include potatoes, sweet corn, tomatoes, and squash. Rhode Island's orchards grow fruits such as apples, peaches, pears, and berries.

Farmers raise different types of livestock, including dairy cows, hogs, and hens. The products that come from the livestock are often processed or prepared in the state. Milk and other dairy products are important agricultural commodities in Rhode Island.

Commercial fishing is not as large an industry as it once was. But fishing boats in

Commercial fishers at work in Narragansett Bay

towns and villages such as Galilee along the Narragansett Bay bring in flounder, cod, tuna, squid, scallops, and whiting. Rhode Island fishers also harvest clams and lobsters.

Rhode Island's seafood industry is threatened by pollution in Narragansett Bay, where most of the state's fishing takes place. The state's old sewage treatment plants are no longer effective. After a heavy rainfall, water tends to fill up the treatment plants, causing an overflow of sewage into the bay. This sewage is harming the fish and other sea creatures, affecting the state's fishing industry, but environmental groups and concerned citizens are working to reduce pollution in the bay.

The Service Industry

To make up for the decline of manufacturing and to help improve Rhode Island's economy, state officials began to try to attract service industries to the region in the 1970s. Today, most of Rhode Island's economy is made up of service jobs, particularly in health care and education. About 20 percent of the state's workforce is employed in health care or education. The state hopes to make itself a center of these growing fields, which it has dubbed "meds and eds."

The health services industry, the state's largest, includes doctors' offices, hospitals, and walk-in clinics. In 2011, Brown University opened a new medical school (the only one in the state) about 1 mile (1.6 km) from its main campus in Providence.

Those who perform educational services, such as teachers and school administrators, also make up a sizable portion of the service industry, as do people who work in finance, insurance, and real estate. Cities such as Providence and

Brown University opened its medical school in 2011.

Warwick host the headquarters for a number of large banks and other financial institutions.

Tourism and the Economy

Tourism is a major contributor to the state's economy. It is also the state's fastest-growing industry. The coastal town of Newport draws people from around the world. Its grand mansions are among its most popular destinations. One mansion, Rosecliff, completed in 1902, was modeled after Versailles, the palace of kings in France.

Newport's Cliff Walk offers stunning ocean views. In the heart of Newport is the Brick Market Place, filled with shops and restaurants. Nearby is Saint Mary's, the oldest Roman Catholic parish in Rhode Island—it was founded in 1828.

Newport also hosts world-famous sporting events. From 1930 to 1983, it was home to the America's Cup yacht races. Every two years in mid-June, the Newport Bermuda

The Newport Bermuda Yacht Race is a famous sailing event that begins in Newport every two years.

Yacht Race is held. Beginning in Newport, boaters race 635 nautical miles (731 miles, or 1,176 km) across the ocean to the island of Bermuda. For tennis lovers, the International Tennis Hall of Fame on Newport's historic Bellevue Avenue is open to the public.

Ron Blake performs at the Newport Jazz Festival in 2017.

During the summer, Newport's annual jazz, folk, and classical musical festivals attract large crowds and talented performers. The jazz and folk festivals take place at Fort Adams in Newport. The classical musical festival is held in Newport's mansions.

There are many recreational firsts in the state that are connected with Newport. The city hosted the first circus performance in what is now the United States in 1774. The first polo match played in the United States was held there is 1876. Five years later, the city was the site for the first US National Lawn Tennis Championship, a tournament that became what we now know as the US Open. The United States Golf Association held the first US Amateur Championship and the first US Open Championship at Newport Golf Club in 1895.

Several nights a year, Providence hosts WaterFire. About eighty sparkling bonfires are set ablaze in baskets along three rivers that pass through the middle of the capital city. History lovers are often found on Providence's Benefit Street. Stephen Hopkins's home is located near Benefit Street. Hopkins signed the Declaration of Independence and was Rhode Island's colonial governor from 1755 to 1767.

South of Providence is Warwick—Rhode Island's third-largest city. Warwick is known as the retail capital of Rhode Island. Warwick is also home to Rhode Island's main airport, T. F. Green International Airport.

The Mushroom King

Though Rhode Island does not have a lot of room to grow crops, tax benefits have brought new opportunities in agriculture. Mushroom farming is just one of those new opportunities.

Mushroom farmer Mike Hallock has been dubbed "Rhode Island's Mushroom King."

Hallock's business, RI Mushroom Co., grows rare mushrooms in West Kingston and sells them to local restaurants and big stores, like Whole Foods.

Since it began in 2013, Hallock's company has grown quickly. RI Mushroom Co. sells nearly 40,000 pounds (18,144 kg) of mushrooms every week. In 2018, to expand his business, Hallock submitted a $115 million proposal to the state government to create an Agricultural Innovation Campus at the University of Rhode Island. Hallock's was one of sixteen proposals for an innovation campus received by the state, including some from major companies like IBM and Johnson & Johnson. The new facility would be a huge boost to the local economy. It's also proof of the innovative ideas that come from Rhode Island.

Mike Hallock's company, RI Mushroom Co., is creating new job opportunities for Rhode Islanders.

Farther south, ferries transport people from the fishing village of Galilee to Block Island. The island's quaint inns and serene beaches are not the only draws. Each fall, bird-watchers come to see songbirds that stop on the island on their journey south.

Those wanting to "spin" around Rhode Island can check out the state's many merry-go-rounds. Built in 1876, the Flying Horse Carousel in Westerly may be the oldest in the country. The twenty hand-carved wooden horses are suspended from chains and swing, or "fly out," as the carousel turns.

The Flying Horse Carousel in Westerly has been a fun family attraction since it was built in 1876.

A New Beginning

Thanks to the efforts of Rhode Islanders, the state's economy is changing and growing. Rhode Island offers great tax incentives to bring in new businesses to the state, and new industries are taking hold. These new companies are helping Rhode Island to bounce back after the recession. In fact, the state's economy looks better and better every year. It is estimated that by 2024, Rhode Island will have thirty thousand new jobs for its residents.

The Rhode Island State
House opened in 1904.

5 Government

It's important to understand how Rhode Island's government works. The government makes big decisions that affect all Rhode Islanders, and it's never too early to get involved. Like the rest of the United States, Rhode Island has two main political parties: the Democratic Party and the Republican Party. Overall, Rhode Islanders tend to vote "blue," or for Democratic candidates. Yet all of Rhode Island's politicians work hard to do what they think is best for the Ocean State.

The History of Rhode Island's Government

Rhode Island once had five state capitals—one for each county. In 1854, the number was reduced to two: Providence and Newport. In 1900, Providence became the sole capital.

Rhode Island adopted a state constitution to replace its old royal charter in 1843. After that, the constitution was changed, or amended, more than forty times. Amendments to the constitution must be approved first by a majority vote in both houses of the state legislature,

FAST FACT

In 2014, Gina Raimondo became the first woman to be elected governor of Rhode Island. Originally from Smithfield, Raimondo attended Harvard University, Oxford University, and Yale Law School before entering politics.

Gilbert Stuart painted more than one hundred portraits of George Washington, including this one. One of Stuart's portrait hangs in the Rhode Island State House.

followed by a majority vote of the people in an election. In 1986, an updated version of the constitution was adopted.

A state constitution describes how a state's government is organized and what powers the government has. A state constitution also limits the powers of government in order to protect the rights of individuals. Like the US Constitution, the Rhode Island constitution divides its government into three separate branches to balance the power of each branch. The executive branch carries out state laws, the legislative branch makes new laws or changes existing ones, and the judicial branch interprets laws.

State Government

A governor, elected to a four-year term, heads the state. Rhode Island is one of the few states that does not have an official governor's residence.

Rhode Island's legislature is called the general assembly. It is made up of two houses, or chambers, a senate and a house of representatives. Senators and representatives represent specific regions of the state.

The state government is responsible for issues that affect the state. The job of state officials includes drafting, approving, and enforcing laws, as well as managing state budgets. The state government also handles issues with other states, as well as with the federal government in Washington, DC.

Rhode Island's state government is centered in its capital, Providence. State lawmakers meet inside the capitol, called the Rhode Island State House. The governor, lieutenant governor, secretary of state, general treasurer, and other officials work here as well.

Building began on the Rhode Island State House in 1895. Inside the building is a vault that contains the Royal Charter of 1663 from King Charles II of England. The charter guaranteed Rhode Island's settlers' freedom of religion and freedom to govern their own colony. Hanging in the Rhode Island State House is a famous painting of George Washington by Rhode Island's Gilbert Stuart.

The Branches of Government

The Executive Branch

The governor heads the executive branch and carries out the laws that the legislative branch passes. He or she is elected every four years and may serve only two terms in a row. Other executive branch officials include the lieutenant governor (who takes over if the governor can no longer serve), attorney general, secretary of state, and general treasurer. Each of these officials is voted into office to serve a four-year term. Like the governor, these elected officials cannot serve more than two terms in a row.

The Legislative Branch

Rhode Island's legislative branch is called the general assembly. It is made up of a senate with thirty-eight members and a house of representatives with seventy-five members. Members of both houses earn their jobs through popular elections, and each serves a two-year term. Rhode Island's general assembly is responsible for making the state's laws and approving people nominated by the governor to be justices of the state's supreme court.

The Judicial Branch

Providence
County Courthouse

Rhode Island's judicial branch interprets and applies the state's laws. The state's highest court is the supreme court. It is made up of a chief justice and four associate justices who serve life terms. The superior court is the state's main trial court. It consists of twenty-two judges whom the governor chooses with the senate's approval. In addition, Rhode Island has family, district, municipal, and probate courts. The governor, with the consent of the senate, appoints these judges. More serious criminal and civil cases are sent to the superior court, which also hears appeals of district court decisions.

Making State Laws

State laws often start out as the ideas of concerned residents. Any Rhode Islander can talk to his or her state legislators about issues that affect the state and its residents. If a resident—or a group of residents—has a suggestion for a new law, it can be presented to a state legislator. Often, the legislator will develop the idea into a bill (a proposed law). The bill is then presented to the legislator's chamber of the general assembly.

If the legislator is a senator, the bill is brought first to the senate. If the legislator is a state representative, the bill is brought to the house of representatives.

The bill gets a specific number to identify it. The numbered bill then goes to a committee of

Rhode Island representatives say the Pledge of Allegiance before getting to work.

legislators for review. The committee members read and discuss the bill. If they agree with it, they can recommend that the bill be passed as it is. If the bill is not recommended, it does not move forward. The committee can also make changes, refer the bill to another committee, or recommend that the discussion of the bill should be postponed. The committee may also present the bill to fellow legislators without comment.

If the bill is recommended for passage, it is discussed by the full senate or full house. Changes may be made or the bill might remain the same. If the legislators of one house approve the bill, it goes to the other chamber for approval. Once there, the bill follows the same process until it is approved. If the senate and the house approve two different versions of the same bill, a conference committee that includes members of both houses meets to resolve the differences. The committee ultimately creates a final version of the bill for approval by both chambers of the general assembly.

A bill that has been approved by both houses in exactly the same form is then sent to the governor. The governor can approve the bill by signing it, and the bill becomes a law. He or she can also allow the bill to become law without

This map shows Rhode Island's five counties.

signing it. If the governor disagrees with the bill, he or she can veto (reject) it. Even if a bill is vetoed, it still has a chance to become law if three-fifths of the members of both houses of the legislature vote again to approve it. This is called overriding the governor's veto.

Municipalities

Rhode Island is divided into five counties: Providence, Kent, Washington, Bristol, and Newport. There is, however, no county government. The main units of local government within the state are its thirty-nine municipalities. They are made up of eight cities and thirty-one towns. The majority of these municipalities are run by a mayor and a city or town council.

As in other states, many towns in Rhode Island hold annual town meetings. These meetings originated during the colonial era, and all eligible voters can attend. At these sessions, voters can approve local spending, pass laws, and even elect local officials.

Representatives in Washington, DC

At the national level, Rhode Island has representatives in both houses of the

Staying Informed

Even if you're too young to vote, you can still get involved in politics. The first step is learning about what's going on in your state. Rhode Island's state government makes it easy to follow along. The official state government website (http://www.ri.gov) provides links to important web pages. One web page contains links to the official social media accounts for the state: http://www.ri.gov/socialmedia. The state government of Rhode Island has a Facebook account and a Twitter account, which are great resources for learning up-to-date information. (Make sure you ask a trusted adult before signing on to social media.)

Once you've learned about issues you care about, you can tell your lawmakers your ideas. Research the addresses of your representatives and write them letters. The first step is to use the "Find Your Elected Officials" tool on http://vote.sos.ri.gov. Enter your home address to find who represents you. Once you know whom you want to write to, you can search for their official website. Writing letters is one way you can shape your government. It's never too early to voice your ideas to the people who are responsible for making and enforcing the laws.

Rhode Island's government website is full of valuable information, including links to the state's official social media accounts.

Members of the US House of Representatives begin their session in January 2017.

US Congress. Each state elects two US senators, who serve six-year terms. There is no limit on the number of terms a US senator can serve. A state's population determines the number of people that it sends to the US House of Representatives. Rhode Islanders elect two representatives to the House. They serve two-year terms and can be reelected an unlimited number of times.

Heading Into the Future

In the summer of 2018, Rhode Island's lawmakers attempted to pass a law that would force presidential candidates to release their tax returns. This law was seen as an attack on President Trump, who has not released his tax returns. Though the bill did not pass, it shows that the Ocean State's politics can have a big impact on national politics. To continue to make a difference, Rhode Island relies on its lawmakers and the active participation of its citizens. Rhode Island has always been known for its leaders, from Roger Williams to the Rhode Islanders of today. It's the hard work of the people that makes Rhode Island so special.

Glossary

climate	The average weather conditions of a particular place or region over a period of years.
coastline	All of the land near a shore, especially along the ocean.
commercial	Of or relating to business or trade.
dialect	The speech patterns of an area.
economy	The way a system of production, trade, and ownership is arranged.
glacier	A large body of ice moving slowly down a slope or valley or spreading outward on a land surface.
immigrant	A person who comes to a country to live there.
Industrial Revolution	The time of transition to new manufacturing processes from about 1760 to 1840.
industry	The businesses that provide a particular product, service, or manufacturing activity.
longhouse	A long dwelling for several families.
mansion	A large home with many rooms.
manufacturing	To make a product from raw materials by hand or using machines.
Native Americans	People who lived on the North American continent before the arrival of Europeans.
population	The whole number of people living in a country or region.
reservation	An area of lands set aside especially for use by Native Americans to continue to live by tribal laws and rights.
settler	A person who makes a home in a new region.
tourism	The industry that supports people traveling for business or for fun.

Wallum
Lake
Slatersville
Woonsocket
Pawtucket
Reservoir
Casimir
Pulaski
Memorial
State Park
Pascoag
Mapleville
Slatersville
Reservoir
Manville
Abbott Run
Valley
102
Pascoag
Reservoir
Woonsocket
Reservoir
Blackstone River
Chepachet
44
Harmony
Stillwater
Reservoir
Lincoln Woods
State Park
Valley Falls
126
Smith and
Sayles
Reservoir
Waterman
Reservoir
Greenville
Saylesville
Pawtucket
Jerimoth
Hill
Ponaganset River
Johnston
Providence
East
Providence
6
Woonasquatucket R.
295
Foster
Moosup
Valley
Scituate
Reservoir
Cranston
Meshanticut
State Park
1
ALT
1
103
Haines Memorial
State Park
Barrington
102
Moosup River
Pawtuxet River
West
Warwick
Quidnick
Warren
114
Warwick
Bristol
Mount
Hope
Bay
Flat River
Reservoir
Coventry
East
Greenwich
Greenwich
Bay
Goddard
Memorial
State Park
Providence River
Wood River
Quidnessett
Narragansett
Bay
PRUDENCE
ISLAND
24
Stafford
Pond
Tiverton
Island
Park
Portsmouth
81
Exeter
Beaver River
Queen River
Plum
Point
CONANICUT
ISLAND
114
AQUIDNECK
ISLAND
Hope Valley
Hundred Acre
Pond
Chipuxet River
138
Middletown
Sakonnet River
77
Quicksand
Pond
95
Pawcatuck River
Great
Swamp
138
Kingston
Jamestown
Newport
Fort Adams
State Park
Sachuest Point
National
Wildlife
Refuge
Sakonnet
Ashaway
Narragansett
Indian
Reservation
Indian
Cedar
Swamp
Peacedale
Worden
Pond
Point
Judith
Pond
Narragansett
RHODE ISLAND SOUND
Royal Indian
Burial
Ground
Westerly
Bradford
Watchaug
Pond
Charlestown
Green Hill
Pond
Fishermen's
Memorial
State Park
ATLANTIC OCEAN
Ninigret
Pond
Quonochontaug
BLOCK ISLAND SOUND
Watch Hill
Sand Dunes
miles
0   4
Block Island
National
Wildlife
Refuge
N
W   E
S
Great Salt
Pond
BLOCK
ISLAND

Interstate
Highway
U.S.
Highway
State
Highway
State
Capital
City or
Town
Indian
Reservation
Swamp
Wildlife
Refuge
Highest Point
in the State
State Park
Sand Dunes

Map Skills

1. What is Rhode Island's capital, and how is it marked on the map?

2. What ocean borders Rhode Island?

3. What town is found on Conanicut Island?

4. What is the highest point in the state?

5. Which direction would you travel to get from Warwick to Providence?

6. What point of interest is south of Westerly?

7. What direction is Peacedale from Kingston?

8. What state park is on Aquidneck Island?

9. Which US highway connects Providence and Chepachet?

10. Which interstate runs north-south in the center of the state?

Answers:

1. Providence, by a star
2. The Atlantic Ocean
3. Jamestown
4. Jerimoth Hill
5. North
6. Watch Hill Sand Dunes
7. South
8. Fort Adams State Park
9. Route 44
10. I-95/295

More Information

Books

Doak, Robin. *Exploring the Rhode Island Colony*. Exploring the 13 Colonies. New York: Smithsonian, 2016.

Heinrichs, Ann, and Matt Kania. *Rhode Island*. U.S.A. Travel Guides. North Mankato, MN: The Child's World, 2017.

Yomtov, Nel. *Rhode Island*. My United States. New York: Scholastic, 2018.

Websites

Kids Zone
http://sos.ri.gov/divisions/Civics-And-Education/kids-zone
The Rhode Island secretary of state hosts this website just for kids. Find interesting facts about Rhode Island, games, and activities.

The Narragansett Indian Tribe
http://narragansettindiannation.org
Learn more about the Narragansett Indian Tribe on their official website.

Rhode Island: The Ocean State
https://kids.nationalgeographic.com/explore/states/rhode-island/#rhode-island-landscape.jpg
Explore facts about Rhode Island's history and geography on this site from National Geographic Kids.

Visit Rhode Island
https://www.visitrhodeisland.com
The official tourism website for the state of Rhode Island includes a calendar of events, information about attractions, and more.

Index

Page numbers in **boldface** refer to images. Entries in **boldface** are glossary terms.